Dear Reader,

Please be advised this book contains some Strong Language that may not be suitable for any persons under the age of 18.

The ♥ Of A Pastor
The Of A Man

Andre' L. Smith

The Heart Of A Pastor, The Pen Of A Man
By: Andre' L. Smith

Cover Created and Designed by: Jazzy Kitty Publishing
Logo Designs by: Andre M. Saunders/Leroy Grayson
Editor: Andre' L. Smith
Co-Editor: Anelda L. Attaway

© 2015 Andre' L. Smith
ISBN 978-0-9916648-9-4
Library of Congress Control Number: 2015938037

All rights reserved. This book is protected under the copyright laws of the United States of America. No part of this publication may be reproduced or transmitted in any format or by any means electronic, mechanical, or otherwise, including photocopying, recording or any other storage or retrieval system without written permission of the publisher, except in the case of brief quotations embodied in critical articles or reviews. For Worldwide Distribution. Printed in the United States of America. Published by Jazzy Kitty Greetings Marketing & Publishing LLC dba Jazzy Kitty Publishing utilizing Microsoft and Adobe Publishing Software. Please be advised this book contains some Strong Language that may not be suitable for any persons under the age of 18.

ACKNOWLEDGMENTS/DEDICATIONS

First and foremost to my Heavenly Father

Thank you Father for giving me the courage to write this book "outside of the box"! Most importantly, thank you for loving me when I couldn't love myself, I Love You more than words could ever say!

To My Wife Dana

You are a precious gift from God, and I thank you for sticking with me through the ugly! Now we Rise!! I love You!

To Mom and Dad

I could not have done this without all of your prayers, encouragement, support and love! You guys are a gift from God, and I love you dearly!

To Gannny Bev and Pop

I Love You. Thank you for your prayers!

To Mike, Marcus, Marvin

I love you guys! Never stop dreaming! Just remember to always keep God first in your life and you will achieve every dream!

To Byron Sr., Missy, Menika, Rayford & Family

I love yall! Thanks for never giving up on me! God answers Prayers!

To Mike C.

Well my brother, here it is finally! Looks like I'll be dropping back off that Trophy, so you better get busy! Love Ya!!

To DTE Family

The Gospel Of Inclusion…Now do you get it? Of course you do!! I Love You Guys! Thank you for allowing me to be versatile with no judgement! Get Ready For God To Move Supernaturally!! 222 (Can You Feel Me?)

To Dr. Downing, Mrs. Cooper, Dr. Shah

Thank you so much for all the words of encouragement and the supply of tissues that you guys kept handy whenever things got tough for me! (Lol) I love you guys…You are the best!!

To Stephanie, Sunny, Cheryl, Lester, Pat, Rodney & Lyons PTSD Staff

I thank all of you for your words of encouragement, laughter, love and genuine care and concern not just for me, but for each and every Combat Veteran that enters the Program! If I had my way, I'd get you guys a raise! Well, I take that back because the reality is, the Govt. couldn't afford that much, it would definitely cause a worldwide deficit! I love you guys… You guys are PRICELESS!

A Special Thank You:

Unok P., Kimberly C., F. Renee S.

TABLE OF CONTENTS

Introduction i
Chapter 1 01
    The Infected Reflection! 01
    You Really are a King 03
    The Complexity of a Warrior 05
    Can it Ever Be Repaired? 07
    God, Help Me to Put on the Brakes. 09
    Back to the Basics! 10
Chapter 2/Love Never Fails!! 12
    I Am Favored 13
    When True Love Strikes 15
    Love is All We Need 16
    Invisible Shredder 17
    I Was Not Created for This! 19
    Only When You Stop and Listen 21
    Partner for Life 23
    When God Shows Up 25
Chapter 3/Not Loving Myself and Partly Loving God 27
    Twisted Twin 28
    I'm Coming Out! 29
    In a World of My Own 31

TABLE OF CONTENTS

Chapter 4/The Program 33
    M.Y.O.B 34
    It's Not Your Turn to Speak 36
    The Concrete Fireplace 37
    Dr. Rainman 39
    Dr. Rainman (2) 40
    Arrest the Med Makers 42
    The Person Behind The Trigger 45
    Who Am I 47
    Can You Feel Me? 48
    About the Author 51

INTRODUCTION

This Book is about Me, Andre' Lamont Smith. Apostle, Pastor, Husband, Father, Combat Soldier (diagnosed w/PTSD), Drug User, Overcomer!!

I've decided, under the guidance of the Holy Spirit to finally let go, and write this book. At the conclusion of it, I will be as free as never before, and if you can identify with any of the poems that are contained within these pages, you will become as free as me. Many of you that will purchase and read this book will call it a travesty. Many will question my relationship with God, and some will even write me off as a phony and a hypocrite; so right now, for all of you that I just described, I say this prayer...Father, please forgive those that have spoken negative things about me after having read this book. They truly do not understand my heart and my relationship with you. Give them the deep understanding and hidden mysteries of Your Words that are contained in each and every piece of literature that I have written. Let them see beyond some of the "strong language" the real Me, which is the Spiritual Being that is completely tied up and entwined in you. Bless them financially for purchasing this book, for their purchase is a financial blessing to Me, your servant. Most importantly, please lead and guide them into a deep, covenant relationship with you through your Son and my Savior, Jesus The Christ. Thank you for answering my prayers as you always have, I Love You. Your Son and Servant, Andre.

Now, for the rest of you that truly understand the Struggle that true Believers face on a day to day basis, as Paul talked about in the book of Romans, this book will be like a breath of fresh air to you. You will no longer feel like you're all alone in your struggles. Moreover, you will know that there are truly anointed Apostles, Bishops, Prophets, Evangelists, and Pastors that are going through tough times just like you, if not worse, and God has maintained His steadfast love for them and has brought them out, just like He's going to bring you out! This book was not written for the faint of Heart, neither was it written for the "Super Christian Leader Who thinks that they can do "no wrong", or that if you use "strong language" at times, that you are not where you should be in your relationship with God. This Book was written by Me, most of which was written after I became ordained and Consecrated as an Apostle. I had some serious struggles, and it was during those times that God allowed Me to express my innermost feelings, thoughts and fears without being judgmental. After which, He would speak to my very Spirit through what I had written, and always allowed Me to see a glimpse of Himself, letting Me know that regardless of what I was going through, that He was, and would remain right there with Me until things got better. I really Love Him For That!

So, if you are a Pastor or Leader of any sort in the Body Of Christ and you are going through some tough times right now, you're not crazy, unsaved, or any of that other stuff that satan is telling you about yourself right now. He is a liar! He always has been, and always will be, so don't believe him! I want you to know this, YOU ARE COMING OUT AS PURE GOLD!! GOD WILL COMPLETE THE GOOD WORK THAT HE BEGAN IN YOU SO LONG AGO! DON'T GIVE UP ON GOD, BECAUSE HE WILL DEFINITELY NOT GIVE UP ON YOU! God Loves You, and So do I! Now, I'm about to begin with some of my poetry for Christian Combat Soldiers! Thank You For Your Service, Men and Women Of God In Uniform! I appreciate You, and just like some of you, I have been diagnosed with P.T.S.D., so I understand your plight. But You do need to know this…It's all under the blood, the Shed Blood of our Lord and Saviour, Jesus The Christ. Now, hold on a sec, while I grab me a "silver bullet" out of the deep freezer, Lol. You, Enjoy!! God Bless

CHAPTER 1

This first poem was written about a week after I arrived at the P.T.S.D. Residential Program in Lyons, New Jersey in 2011. It was the first time that I had begun to see myself. I was a Believer, true enough but I was really screwed up. Most of all, I was very angry at myself, and at that time, I felt like if I could have reached my foot around, and kicked my own butt, I definitely would have! So here it goes…It's called, **"The Infected Reflection!"**

The Infected Reflection!

In front of Me hangs a glass, It's a mirror and it asks me to tell me what it is that I see? I see a Tall, Dark and Handsome King looking back at Me. But that's not all y'all; I see a man that has been injected, infected with the images of War in His mind, that is struggling to find a sense of peace with everyday life, where pain and strife cease to exist…A serene place amidst a group of human beings that are seeing things in life just a little bit in the same way that I do. It's true that we are born differently, shaped uniquely in the image of God…But it's hard to see myself at times as a product of Him, when other humans like me are the cause of making phlegm build up in my throat. Very painful that at certain times others make me sick, but reality tells me that it's just a trick of my greatest enemy...The injected, infected other side of Me! I don't want you to miss this or get this twisted into being something that it's not, so I'm going to stop and give it to you one more time...

There is a King trapped in my mind, and at times He cannot find his way out. He's trapped amidst horrors that cause him to scream out at night; frightened by terrors of His past, believing that one day everything will pass before he's watching the casket close over his face. Every day, He's making a mad dash living life as victoriously as he can, helping himself and others to understand the undeniable, irrefutable effects of his poisoned, war-stained mind. On the other hand, there stands a King, who is excited about everything that life brings his way. He starts each day with a smile that lights up the darkest room; that destroys gloom and grief

With the mere flashing of his teeth! Yeah, this is the King that shows up, stands fast, and grabs a hold of brothers and sisters that are trapped within the dungeons and confines of their minds! Like a knight in shining armor, he disarms the clamor of destructive chatter that they could never seem to bring under control...He does it with such poise and ease that when they're told to take it easy, there is nothing there to put at ease! He leaves and they're left standing being pleased with the King that just disarmed all of their objections. This is the oxymoronic life of the King with the Infected Reflection...Looking back at Himself.

So listen up! Don't get it twisted, **"YOU Really Are A King",** is the title of this next piece. It's especially for you...a poem that should stir up your inner greatness!!

You Really Are A King

With the way things are going on in today's world, it's real easy to miss it, or get it twisted about the man you really are! You see, because you're not a star on M.T.V. or B.E.T. And you haven't won an Emmy or Grammy, and you're just a Christian man providing for your family, the World says you're not successful; yeah, simply because you don't have a desk full of antique, expensive bookends and paperweights...a sterling silver stickman swinging back and forth on top of a diamond studded, solid gold desk clock so you won't be late for your next meeting. A model for a secretary coming in your office feeding you grapes for lunch off of a silver platter, taking care of all of your personal matters...They say that if you don't have a life like this, you really don't have anything...But they got it twisted because you really are a King! Here's why: One day a King that always was, was born. He was then scorned, His skin was torn off of His body ruthlessly as His Family, Friends and Followers watched helplessly as all of this was taking place. This King gave up His life for the entire Human race, and with drops of blood streaming down His face, His concern was for You and Me! Not for us just to live, but to take part in His Kingship, yeah, so that you and I could live Kingly...He infused us with His royalty! He put eternity inside of us...Without a fuss, He gave us the Power here on Earth to make a difference. See, it doesn't make sense to those that are not connected; You are a King, even if you are not respected by those that think they know...In you lies the Power to show the World what being successful is all truly all about! You don't have to shout or boast about having your name being amongst America's Top listed; Naw, see, the got it twisted, Your Kingship didn't come from this World, It came from God! Yeah, don't ever forget, It was God that made You a King...Now walk in it!!

That picture that I just painted for you probably has you nodding your head and saying, "that's me". If so, than you definitely are on your way to complete healing because now you've recognized and distinguished the strongest part of yourself, which is God inside of You. Let me be the first to tell you though, it's all good! You are right where you need to be in order for your Healing process to begin taking effect. So now you ask, what next? Well, this next poem is one of my favorite pieces because it represents the "Caged Me" finally being released! Beloved, read this next piece as fast and as emphatically as you can, and as you do, you will feel yourself breaking out of your self-imposed cage! Trust me; this is truly your New Beginning!!! The poem is entitled **"The Complexity of a Warrior"**

The Complexity of a Warrior

Raging...Raging like a lion that's caged in a steel cage with no way out, Raging...I'm raging, enraged cuz I'm flipping page after page in my mind every time and situation that I gave in, gave up to something self-destructive...Raging, cuz I just did the same thing that I vowed I'd never do...Caged in my emotions, with the notion that I can't be conquered...Yet consumed with bad news brought to me like a courier, this is the mind of a raging warrior!! Raging...Yes, I'm raging inside because I cannot hide the real me that continues to falter; I won't halt or, stop to even take an inventory to address

All of the history from a shattered, tattered past that upstaged me so many times before...Raging, raging as I see me on some floor, behind some door, on my knees calling out to God saying please help me to get it straight and get my life back...while still searching for the smallest piece of crack to stick back in my gear and melt it down...I'm raging, still raging while I'm hearing the sound of a sizzle...Puzzled by the thoughts of what the hell is driving me, to continue this insanity repeatedly over and over again...I'm raging cuz I feel like I have no friends, yet I've been a friend to many...Is there anybody that can feel what I'm saying? But the time has now come to turn this shit cycle around for my good...Raging...

I'm raging, but flipping the page and looking forward to my future...Raging, running fast to suture the wounds of past memories...Raging to Fight against the disease of self-inflicted wounds...I assume responsibility of my actions daily...I'm raging now, barely remembering the dark past and at last I can finally say this...I'm raging and caged in raging and let out, raging on the stage of life, rip roaring to a new beginning!! Yeah, I'm a raging, roaring lion, on my way to a new beginning! Raging, I'm raging, rip roaring and soaring high to success, sleeping in the best hotels like the Waldorf Astoria...

This is the mind and complexity of a raging, rip roaring warrior…A warrior let out of the cage, raging to flip the page to upstage all of those that oppose the way of the cross…Toss me the keys to the cage, so I can lock it for good!! Yeah, never caged in again, the cage is locked for good!!

Yeah!! Every time I read that poem I get strengthened!! Listen, sometimes in life, you will be the only true encourager that you have! You have to learn how to encourage yourself! The lack of joy in your life is the beginning of problems. Trust me, I've been there. I know what it feels like when all of the joy and happiness that you once had feels like it has been sucked out of you!! There is nothing left except pain, bitterness and anguish. This is the exact moment that you must tell yourself to be happy, and then do something about it to get you there! Read a book, tell yourself a joke, read your favorite poem, quote a bible scripture out loud, do something! If you don't, rest assured that you will be heading towards a dark, deep place that you may not ever be able to recover from. Which leads me to the next poem, entitled **"Can It Ever Be Repaired?"**

Can It Ever Be Repaired?

Can my once loving and caring heart ever be repaired back to its natural state? Or now, must I forever face the fate that part of me will never be intact...The heart in me that once shed light has now faded to black...Can it ever be repaired back to its natural state? Or has my black heart initiated a hostile takeover...Making me over from head to toe as a new creature...which my only purpose in life now would be to serve as a monstrous creature in a feature movie starring me as myself as the person who once was...I'm stopping now, taking a pause, crying out to you God, the one that sits on high...look at my eyes as I cry out to you for an answer...Can it ever be repaired? Because the truth is I'm scared of this dark, marred me! Can I be repaired and prepared for the next life that you created for me? Fix me for your purpose, if for nothing else you deserve this, Yeah, you deserve to see destruction shaped into destiny, beauty formed from calamity, a broken damaged dark heart, now made new and set free...All by the work of your hands! Repaired, Renewed, Set Free!! Yeah, the day is coming when you'll repair me! Until then, I will only believe.

You know, one thing that I've realized is that if you truly want to be repaired, you must slow down! Sometimes, we want things to be fixed or changed all at once. The problem with this is that we miss the process, and because of that, we repeat the same mistakes over and over again. This is why we must slow down and embrace the process of change. This brings us into the poem entitled, **"God, Help Me To Put On The Brakes"**

God, Help Me To Put On The Brakes

Just like a Benz pulling out of the dealership gate and I have to stop and wait, look both ways before I turn on the road…God help me to put on the brakes. My life is spinning out of control, this ain't new news, naw, this shit is old, yeah the same old shit that has been happening for years…tears streaming down my face, my mind keeps trying to erase and forget about the mistakes that I've made in the past…Faster and faster my thoughts take me back to the black past that I thought was gone…Faster and Faster Time passes on from the day that I was born, yet I've accomplished nothing…Nothing of noteworthiness, nothing that shows the best of me of what God has created me to be…How much more of this can I take? God please help me to put on the brakes, Dammit! I just wanna put the brakes on. Even if not eternally, just momentarily…just long enough for me to take a deep breath without moving…I want to stand still and allow you to fill my emotional, Psycho-social, spiritual cup until it Runs over…Moreover, I want to camp out by the lake of the still waters while you restore my soul…Yeah,

I will one day sit by the lake, but it won't happen unless you help me to put on the brakes…So God, please help me to put the brakes on, because I'm counting on you…I'm only counting on You!!

The good thing about putting on the "brakes" is that when it's all said and done, you are now ready to run in the race of life and WIN!! It is then that you can go back to the basics and win, because truly you were born to Win!! Check out this poem, **"Back To The Basics!"**

Back To The Basics!

Back to the basics where winning is the norm, I whether every storm…got my Asics on…I'm beginning again, but this time is different, this time I win and health and wealth are now in my hands…I've taken command of my destiny, and the best of me subdues the rest of me right in the middle of my own resistance…Persistence has finally paid off, and now yeah, right now I'm at the top of my game…but I'm standing at the back of the line…this is where two minds meet and collide into something Great…They begin to collaborate and elaborate on a subject that no one else knows…No one except God!! Go in, get in, go fast, go hard, don't stop, fear not, stay straight, don't wait for anyone else to catch up...cuz that's where you messed up the last time, time before that times ten...Your victory is assured, it already began the moment you said "I Do"...So get back to the basics, throw away the Asics and grab you some Nike's for this place...Yeah, there's no more race, no more race, for you are victorious...And the place where you are standing is Holy Ground!! Yeah, Nike's and all, triangles shining...Where the two of us stand, is all Holy Ground!!

CHAPTER 2

Love Never Fails!!

Many of you, like me, have experienced failed relationships, marriages, and have blamed yourself totally for the failures because of the frame of thinking which says, "because you are the man in the relationship and God holds you accountable, it was therefore up to you to make things work"! Well, this is partly true, however not in that exact context. Here's what I mean…Truly, we are called to be the leaders in our homes and in our marriages and relationships, however serving God MUST be our first priority! "Thou shalt have no other Gods before Me." (Exodus 20: 3-5) Unless you allow God to be first in your life, everything else will eventually fail and/or crumble! But the good news is this, when you serve God with your "entire being", you will find out that regardless of whatever "storm" that you face, you will have peace! It may not seem like it at first but trust me, if you just hang in there, I promise you, things will get better! Now, I want to talk about love. God is love, and having someone to love is truly an awesome thing, especially when you allow God to send that "special someone" to you! Yeah, I know brothers, sometimes we get impatient and we go after the first "baam, pow, oooh, cover girl" that we see, only to realize later that the contents are nothing like the "cover"! Lol! This is why it is important, rather crucial for you to wait on God for your "virtuous woman"! As you have read and probably picked up on in the last poem, I believe that true love in a relationship is necessary for true Godly success! This is of course, my opinion, but it is based on the biblical truth that Eve was created for Adam to help and assist him in managing the Garden that God created. Having said that, this chapter will contain many of the love poems that I wrote during some of my most difficult times in life. Although, some were "person" specific at that time, all were God (love) generated, so He gets the glory for them! Thanks Dad for teaching me how to truly love and appreciate love...I love you! And because you love me, I know that I am, and have always been Favored in your eyes!

I Am Favored

The labor by which I was made lets me know that I am favored...Spoken by words that were savored inside of my Heavenly Father before time ever began. Yeah, it was always a part of a universal plan to make and bring out the best in me. After He created the land and the sea, the stars and the moon, He spooned me up out of the depths of His Spirit and spoke me into existence...and that's the reason for the resistance that I face on a daily basis from the enemy! Because I am favored, and he sees and knows exactly what I was created to do...the true, blue me; sent on assignment by G.O.D. to free all of those that are trapped within the confines of their own minds. Trapped like in a jungle on a deserted island...like in a cave or, I can't even fathom because I'm Fa-vored! Yeah, favor follows me, surrounds me, amazes me...God's favor brings my destiny into a reality that just simply blows my mind! His favor is one of a kind, and it kind of makes me wonder, whenever I hear the thunder, is more of His favor being released to me? Undoubtedly, I have been made in His image and after His likeness...Yeah, just imagine this, I am made in the image of God! This is why it's not so hard to see myself as someone who is Amazing...Even on the days that I cannot reach my peaceful core, I am reminded of the favor that I have been given...so I keep on living because God made me; and because He made me, I am forever favored...Yeah, for all eternity, I am and will always be, Forever Favored!

Wow, right? Being Favored and loved by God is Awesome! It truly is the best thing that can happen to anyone, but sometimes it's necessary to feel and experience love from another human being, other than your family, of course. Yeah, love from the Woman of your dreams can make you feel... (Lol)! Check this out, this is what I felt when love from my True Love, struck Me!! I Love You Dana!!!

When True Love Strikes

When true love strikes, it's like your heart is always beating at a rapid pace, even when you're standing face to face with them in their presence...The pure essence of love arises as you stare into their eyes and enjoy the bliss of the moment...You deliver a kiss of atonement letting her know that all of her faults are forgiven, then you lean in, and you begin to kiss her again and again until both of your love meters spike...This is what happens when true love strikes!! Yeah, when true love strikes, it's like nothing else really matters, because her love begins to heal your bruised, battered, shattered past until you become whole. No more cold kisses on your lips, instead her hips are in your lap as she sits and leans back to whisper in your ear... Yeah, in case you're wondering, this poem here, is about my dear beautiful wife Dana...And there ain't a thing you haters can do about it, so you might as well step off and take a hike, cuz this is what you see when true love strikes! Yeah, when true love strikes, its like...Umm, I can't share that with you, you're too nosey! So, just go dry off and find your own!* **Love Is All We Need**, is the next piece. Check this out:

Love Is All We Need

From the time we were formed in our Mother's womb, God gave us a gift called love. It was harnessed in His hands, perfected with His presence, and poured out from the Heavens above. He gave us this gift so we could share with one another, every woman, every child and man. With the sole purpose being, to spread His salvation, which is His ultimate and unfailing plan. So why do we fail, you may ask yourself, to give love as Christ has instructed? Maybe its because we've forgotten how to love, because our lives are terribly corrupted. Or maybe its because, as we comprehend love, we realize one simple fact; that in giving true love there's always the chance of someone not giving it back. But whatever the reason, the case or the cause, for God's love, our hearts must yearn...See, the timing is crucial, and we must be prepared, on the day of His triumphant return. What must we do, to reserve our place in Heaven where there is no lack or greed; Start by loving God first, then loving all humanity, because that love, is all that we need.

Now what great love relationship doesn't come with quarrels and arguments? None that I know of! As a matter of fact, some people believe that an occasional "good argument" is healthy for any relationship. I don't know if I wholeheartedly agree with that frame of thinking, however I can tell you that I've had my share of arguments, and they never really worked out to well after that! So, that's when I began to transform my feeling of anger into poetry. This is where some of the language might get a little "strong", but the truth is I can almost guarantee that many of you will be shaking your head in agreement and laughter after reading the next two pieces. The first one is called the **Invisible Shredder.** Let me just say this about this poem before I begin…WORDS DO HURT, So be careful as to what you allow yourself to say to another person when you are angry, as well as what words you allow yourself to accept into your Spirit when spoken by someone who is angry at you! Occasional arguments, sporadic arguments, arguments of all sorts may be good for some people, but as for me, I can truly say that **I Was Not Created For This!!** Enjoy!

Invisible Shredder

If I told you to invent a product that would turn your cents into dollars, what on earth would it be? Hmm, let's see, a double-

sided knife, naw, already done. Wait, even better, let me introduce to you, the **Invisible Shredder!**

Invisible Shredder, how could you ever, use something that you cannot see? Well, let me tell you that its real, because it damn sure cut me! At first, like you could only perceive, it stuck me like a pin, but then bit by bit, that shit really started hurtin'... Words and actions suggesting that you were flirtin', messing around with another, Slice! Hey honey, why did you say that, that wasn't so nice! A hug and a kiss to patch up the wound but soon, unexpectedly, from the north of Schenectady, (New York) that is, like cheez whiz shooting out of a can spews out of Her mouth words that cut this man straight to the core. Abhorred with feelings of inadequacy, He thinks how in the world could she be, that mad at me, to say those things with all of the hostility that it brings! Yeah, hostile and violent, but He still remains silent...Slice, Slice! The cut is now deeper, reopened. The tears He can no longer hide, caused by the hurt that He suffers on the inside; and yet He remains still...Silent amidst His own tears trying to heal, year after year. Then it happens, all of a sudden, or so she thinks...But its really a direct result of all of the stink from the horrible words that shredded His heart in half, naw, a third...and that's word! He gets up enough nerve with His fragmented heart, and begins to rebuild what she shredded apart with those words! Yeah, No one thought He'd ever recover, from those sharp ass blades of the Invisible Shredder!

I Was Not Created For This!

As I sit and sip my coffee, think and reminisce; I say out loud, with a grin on my face, I was not created for this! When I was created, people were elated, joy filled the air...As I spent precious moments in the arms of a woman receiving a tender kiss; not fussing and fighting, cussing and yelling, I was not created for this! I miss the spoken prophetic words that I heard when I was just a kid...regardless of the naughty things that I did or got into. Corrections were made, but then it was through, it was over, never spoken of again...the dawn of a new day became my best friend! The start of a brand new day...Wow! What excitement, what heavenly bliss! Not kicking me when I'm down, hell naw, I was not created for this! I WAS NOT CREATED FOR THIS!! See This, this kind of shit will make me ball up my fists and knock the hell out of somebody, anybody, everybody that's around me...the ones that are trying to down me and clown me! I have a Warrior's will, in the Army they armed me, I wasn't taught to fight, only trained to kill...So please don't try to steal my joy, 'cause boy oh boy if you do, If I catch you, yo' ass is thru! Finished, caput, buried and surely missed...so don't play yourself close because I, I was not created for this! I was created from love, by love, to be loved, now are you catching my drift...to change the World with Love, I was created for this!! But some folks get it twisted, yeah, they add their own twist in this drink called life, not a lemon wedge, but a wedge of strife pushed in between what's right and what's wrong...now standing all alone, singing that sad ass song "Woe is me, why did this happen to me?", all defeated and beat down like the Soldiers on the shores of Tripoli! These are the types of people that rarely stop and give a kind word to another, can barely speak correctly, but always talking "slick" to a brother, just 'tryna make themselves look good...Yo, I just wish you could, have a peek at the critters prior to them being exposed to me, then you'd understand first hand, the definition of homely, lonely, living like a "Genie" making wish after wish...to get another chance to live a life like this, full of happiness and bliss; dancing to my tunes entitled "Created For This!" Yeah, I am, and will always be successful, its part of my Divine Nature...So you can be a "Hater", like Mars says "Please hate me, go ahead, I insist!"..."Cuz while you're hating, I've Vaporized...nothing left, not even a mist!" So now you know, how real I was, when I told your stupid ass that I, I WAS NOT CREATED FOR THIS!

I've come to the realization that a lot of arguments and disagreements that are experienced in relationships can be avoided if both parties would just take the time out to really hear what the other person is saying. In order to do that, to "really hear", that is, one must really LISTEN! Not listen while watching the game, on the computer, or doing anything else. Brothers, I know, we get accused of not listening quite often, even though most of the time, we are doing those very things, so their assessment is accurate! Lol! But there are times where you need to communicate something to "Her" and she is not a good listener, so this poem is for the "non-listener"!!

Only When You Stop and Listen

You look at me all puzzled, asking me what is it that is missing? My answer is silence, because you didn't stop and listen! As I told you so many times before, you have to understand and peel back my psychological layers before you can reach my emotional core. Listen to me, see what I see, or at least give it a try...Don't ask why, 'cuz' right now, I don't have an answer. Yeah, this shit has been eating away at me like cancer with no chemo...You don't know what I'm feeling or dealing with on a regular basis! Just to give you an idea, when we go places, I'm looking at people's faces wondering what's going on in their minds...Crazy shit, right? And I haven't even mentioned the fight that I have at night with those dreams that intrude my mind. Yeah, 20/20 hindsight says that I should have just stayed in school...That would have been cool cuz I'd probably be somewhere, In some clinic, at some hospital, helping someone like me to regain some sense of normality in their life. Helping them to reduce stress and strife to a level that is manageable... Tangible results that make my colleagues say "Dre's techniques are bitchin!"...Now do you get it, just stop and listen, to exactly what it is that I'm trying to say to you. I'm dying to tell you the deep truth in my heart, but here lately when I start to reveal the real, raw aspect of the inner me, you interject haphazardly with your own thoughts and emotions. Not seeing that this is a main ingredient of the potion called "lack of proper communication"...Then for the rest of the duration of the conversation I shut down, and the true me is never revealed. I then sit still and listen to try to understand your pain...What's gained is that I now have a better glimpse of the inner you; now I'm apologizing to undue the hurt that was caused by the expression of my feelings, by my feelings expressed? And now, yeah, right now the tears begin to flow once again, my eyes begin to glisten...With the saddening thought but hopeful belief that one day, you'll just stop and listen! Yeah, 'cuz' on that day you will see me as I really am...A King that was birthed and trained in the midst of trouble! A Great King...that God gave to you!

Realization of your "Partner For Life" sometimes happen when you are in your deepest "valley". It is then that they show up with love, grab your hand, and climb up and out with you! They hurt when you hurt, they smile when you smile, and their main objective in life, other than serving God of course, is to make sure that you are always "okay". If you can ever find this person, be smart enough to marry this person, for truly, this person will be your **"Partner For Life"**!

Partner For Life

Craze filled days' time after time...loose cannon my mind flooded filled to capacity, feeling like someone's after me, and its not paranoia...Classes geared to restore ya, mind back to its original state, but as fate would have it you are the you that you've become because of this trauma...Momma's prayers for me filling God's court in Heaven...Seven Days, Seven Ways to see the Hand of God in Creation...Now I station myself to stand still and receive from Him a gift. As I lift my eyes to the hills where my help comes from, its coming from the Lord...While patiently waiting I begin singing chords of "You Did It All For Me". Tension so high, I can feel it...Anger so intense I can see it, I see red in my eyes! Cries of frustration lasting the entire duration of this class...Will this situation ever pass, I ask myself, does it ever get better? It will when I let Her, words penetrate my heart as they came from Her lips..."Honey, I love you, I'm with you, I support you and I've got your back! I will attack those devils that try to confuse you, use you, abuse you, delude you! That's right My King, I've got your back! Today, Tomorrow, Forever...Yeah, I'll Forever have your back!

As I stated earlier, we really cannot comprehend true love with or from another Human Being until we first accept true love at its core, which is the acceptance of God's love for us! Accept it, don't try to understand it, because you can't! God's love transcends our issues, mess ups, hang ups, faults and everything else that we go through in life! See, when God shows up in our "mess", He's not coming to be a part of it, nor did He come to torment or criticize you while you're in it...When God shows up, His desire is to bring you out of it, and lead you into the destiny that you were created for, so just allow Him to do it!

When God Shows Up

When God shows up, He fills my cup until it runs over... Moreover, He sheds light on my night filled days that bring darkness into my soul. He removes it by illuminating my soul with the washing with the water of the Word. He's forever married to me, a marriage with no prenup...peace fills my Spirit when God shows up! Yeah, when God shows up, the pains of my present are pushed to the back of my mind...Stored behind the joy that starts within...When God shows up, He serves as my friend! He listens to all of my cares and concerns. He yearns for me to open up so that He can come in and sup with me, bringing me to a new reality, of His unyielding love for me! Yeah, when God shows up, I'm free to do me, to see what I can't see through the eyes of Faith...Then saith the Lord, I'm here for you, I'm near to you. My Child, present me your cup that I might fill it up with Peace, Praise, Faith, Power and Joy; which will destroy all Doubt, Fear, Anger and Anguish! This is my purpose, Don't you want this? I have come to fill up your cup! Yeah, its time to live in overflow, "cuz" God has shown up! Yes Beloved, when God shows up, He fills your cup up until it runs over, Your Cup Will Run Over…And You'll Live In Overflow!

Life in overflow is a good thing, especially when it is from God! Love is so beautiful…just had to stop a moment and reflect because there were times that not only did I feel like because of my actions that God didn't love me, but I didn't love me! As a matter of fact, I didn't even like me.

CHAPTER 3

Not Loving Myself and Partly Loving God

The next section of the book represents that time in my life where I was struggling with loving myself and partly loving God. This is where many "Christians" will have a problem with this book, but like Steve Harvey often says "let them go ahead and hate you, just don't ever let them stop you from being you!" As a matter of fact, let me say this about Mr. Steve Harvey, I admire him tremendously for all of what he's done comedic ally, but I admire him most for his "real" relationship with God! If more Christians would become truly transparent, church growth in this generation would be unprecedented! So, welcome to the poems that come from the pen of a man, a man that loves God, but didn't allow, at that time, God's love to truly permeate His Heart! You may be Angry, Frustrated, down right mad as hell at yourself, the world, even God, but beloved I promise you this, if you accept God's love by establishing a personal relationship with Jesus the Christ, YOUR LIFE WILL CHANGE FOR THE BETTER!! It may not happen overnight, but I promise you, God's love will change your life! Hang in there, you can and you will make it out!

The Apostle Paul talks about the ongoing conflict that goes

That I'm Out!!" Yeah, Newsflash Bitch!!...
Now that I'm out, I'm going straight to the top! You can bet your bottom dollar, I'm going straight to the top!!

Lol!!! Y'know, I always laugh when I read that poem because the "bitch" that I'm referring to is satan! I know that's not cool...However, I was feeling pretty confident in overcoming my addiction at that point, and I wanted to let him know that he would no longer have authority over me to make me do anything because I was taking back my authority with the help of God and the tools that I was learning from this Program at Lyons, N.J. Let me say this to you, satan is real! And he wants to destroy you, and everything good that exists in you, around you, and that is connected to you; that's real talk! Having said that though, sometimes it's hard to remember that you share your world with others; yeah sometimes you just simply forget. But the reality is that you do, and you share it with those that love you the most, Your Family! Before you start cussing me out about how your family doesn't love you or understand you, let me say this, been there, done that, got the t-shirt. So, for those of you that think or feel that you are in a world of your own, this poem is for you!

In a World of My Own

I'm grown, yeah I'm grown and I can do what I want, I'm in a world of my own! Or am I really? I'd be silly to think that all that I do has no effect on others...My brothers, sisters and family slammed me for my behaviors not only because they love me, but because they're connected! See, I rejected their love and concern because I was selfish...Well this is my life was my constant song...Yeah, I knew I was wrong but I didn't care "cuz" I am grown...A selfish Manchild in a world of my own! Immature for sure, no one to adore but me...Fooled and deceived in a sea of self-absorption...No caution to my actions, thoughts or words...Not believing what I heard, to put it bluntly, I'm living an absurd lifestyle; when all the while I just need to realize that all though I'm grown, my world is not my own, I share it with others...Yeah, brothers, sisters, family and loved ones, I share my life with others! Note To Self...Your World Is Not Your Own!

Yeah, that reality was a hard one for me to accept at first, but when I sat down and really began to think about it, I was then ready to begin to mend some of those bridges that I tore down with my reckless behavior and actions. The truth is, and to my surprise, when they saw that I had come to this realization, they were right there with me to help me put my life back together! I Love all of my family for that, especially my Wife, Children, Mom and Dad!

CHAPTER 4

The Program

This next section of the book deals with the program itself. Now some of the poems when you read them, you will know exactly which class I was in when I was writing, and some of you will laugh and agree wholeheartedly with me. Others might take offense, however I must say this, these poems were not written to offend or upset anyone! They were just my thoughts and feelings at that time and the reason why I'm putting them in this book is because there may be someone feeling the same way but not know how to express it…so these poems are written for their healing, Healing through laughter! The first poem is entitled **M.Y.O.B**. Now this poem was written because during my time in treatment, there was always that one person that always had something to say about everybody else! So, if you encounter this type of person while you are in treatment, or in life just kindly guide them to this page to read this poem. Make sure you do it with kindness and a smile, hopefully they will get the message and begin to focus on their own treatment, but if not, well they will at least know to leave you alone! Lol!

M.Y.O.B.

Talking back, taking in...A friend to many, an enemy to them. They don't know me, they don't have a clue as to who I really am...It's sad because I am from He who is...Mr. and Mrs., please stop judging me, get your own free "cuz" believe it or not, you are a captive of your own self! Wealth has eluded you, fear has corroded you, and small thinking contains you! It is plain to see, can't you see it plainly? Probably not because you are mainly focused on me and what I'm doing...Watching me even when I'm chewing my snuff...Yo, back up homie, enough is enough!! Mind your own business, can you hear this? Yes you, I'm talking to you! Mind your own business and catch this... Focus on your treatment alone, "cuz" when you go home and shit breaks down, you are the only one to blame! It would be a shame for you not to have success...A shear mess that you allowed someone else to affect your treatment to the point that you carried it home with you!! Stand up and be true, yeah be true to yourself that you are nosey...So suppose you do this, Mind your own business you nosey bitch, and just focus on yourself! You only have one life to live, and that life only involves YOU!

Sometimes in treatment, you might find yourself really

wanting to share and open up and let go of some of the stuff that you've been holding in for years, only to be in a class where you don't have the opportunity because the instructor is only concerned that day about getting to you their agenda. If this happens, don't be discouraged! When you get to your trauma group, release it! If your trauma group is days away, find someone to talk to! The staff is there to help you, and even if you can't find someone on staff to talk to, talk to one of the other vets that you've bonded with while being there. If that doesn't work, write it in your "green book"! Whatever you do, just make sure that you get it out of you, because releasing all that stuff is what brings about your Healing! These poems that you are reading right now, I'm copying directly out of my green books…Yeah, I got three of them because I been through the program three times! The first two times, I didn't really get it, and that is why I began writing this book, so that I can help you avoid some of the simple mistakes and mindsets that caused me to have to repeat the program three times. Now don't get me wrong, each time I learned more, grew more, understood more, and even learned how to laugh more, but I could have gotten it the first time around if I read a book like this! Lol! Now, back to the poetry stuff! I wanted to share in this particular class on this particular day and there was a "newbie" staff member. I don't think anyone told her that "we" have a lot to share. She was putting out some good info, but she wouldn't let anyone get a word in edgewise…well so she thought! I just whipped out my book and began to speak with my pen on paper, and this is what I wanted her to know…**It's Not Your Turn To Speak!** Enjoy…

It's Not Your Turn To Speak

Every week, we come in, rearrange seats and then you begin to speak. We sit and listen with a meek and humble spirit, trying to really hear it…Yeah, hear exactly what it is that you're trying to say…Trying to take in concepts that will help us to live better lives day by day, but then you keep right on talking…Its like caulking a window that has already been sealed, an overload of information like an unwanted meal, so listen up now, here is the real deal…Sometimes, you just need to feed us a little info at a time, then let us answer and unwind the emotions that we have pinned up inside…Try not to interrupt when the vets start talking, let them walk you into their emotional core…A place that even they have never been before, so keep your mouth shut so that the door of their soul remains open. This is how they cope with and deal with their P.T.S.D…This is how they break free and move into a new, higher self! So please take this wealth of information that I'm passing along to you, sometimes simply shutting up is the best teaching that you can do...Yeah, just sit back, shut up, and listen! Then you'll be able to see the real difference that you're one hour class made!

As I mentioned earlier, your Trauma Group will become your best friend while you're in treatment if you allow it to be! This is where you can truly let go of all the hurtful, painful things that you did to others, and that happened to you in your life! Especially if you served at any point in theatre! This next poem was inspired by a Marine that I met while in the program twice. He served in Vietnam, and he taught me a lot while I was there in Lyons. The funny thing was that he didn't say to much outside of Trauma Group, but while in Trauma Group, He taught me, and many others how to really jt open up and "let it go"! L. J., I'll always thank you for teaching me how to release and throw my "shit" into the Trauma Group Room, known as the **"Concrete Fireplace!"**

The Concrete Fireplace

It's a race to release the feelings in the concrete fireplace...The place where hurtful things are burned up, feelings that have been pinned up inside for a very long time...The hurtful things in my mind that caused me to isolate, living a fate that I thought had no answer…Eating at me like a cancer from the inside out…Yeah, talking to myself, pleading my own case to release all of my trauma into the concrete fireplace!

It's time to let it go, time to throw it all in, but where does one begin? The trend is to bend, then break and send, these inward Demons to a fiery end…Toss it in to the Concrete Fireplace, and just in case you don't because of fear, just look around you at all of the faces that are trying to do the same thing…they're bringing up real, raw emotions mixed with tears that make up a potion of guilt and depression. There is a lesson to be learned, a joy to be found, loose ends to tie up like a shoelace…but it can only be accomplished when you let go and toss your shit into the concrete fireplace…Yeah, just like L.J. said "You're around family, so just toss your shit into the concrete fireplace…"cuz" at the end of the day, it's all about YOUR HEALING!"

Here is another poem I wrote while sitting in class, angry about the lesson being taught, but what's different about this one is that there is a Part 2 to it also. I will tell you that after writing part two, my treatment got a whole lot better. It wasn't because the training was different, the materials were different or even the instructors were different. What was different was my attitude, and the way that I began to look at the program. Like me, you will find progress in the program when you process the program differently in your mind. Trust me, the program begins to work the moment you process it as a positive in your mind!

"Dr. Rainman"

Welcome to the class, pass the clipboard around and sign your name...as he begins spewing the same old shit as usual...How to use your tools and all the other shit that you've gotten to fight against triggers...Bigger and Bigger are the troubles that the triggers bring when they remain uncontrolled...by the way, how old are you Doc? "cuz" before I knock down the wall of my emotions and let you in, I gotta know that you're in it all the way...Just cuz you say what you say doesn't validate you... Do you Pray? Huh? I said do you pray? Telling me to believe in my higher power when you're just waiting for Happy Hour to go and share my shit with your colleagues...I pour out until I'm bleeding and you take it in and begin feeding it to them for answers...this is why I just dance or, just don't answer when I'm sitting in your class...I'm just penning my shit as I watch the time pass by rapidly...It's two o'clock, now I happily arise from my seat to go to the next class to complete my day of training...but first I have to dry of from the rain...Yeah, it's raining bullshit, and I gotta dry off! Dr. Rainman made it rain again...Now I just gotta go and dry off!!

Dr. "Rainman" (Part 2)

Maybe I was too hard on Him...allowing my scars to scar him with the venom spewing out of my mouth. Southward thinking of people and things spring up and cause words to flow over my tongue...Young and immature actions place factions and sanctions on his teaching style, when all the while I should be paying attention. Not to mention that he's here teaching me for my good, so what I should do is look up, sit still, put away the paper and quill and gather in all that he's giving...It's gonna help me to keep living, yeah, I'm gonna keep on living, going and growing to be the best me that I was created to be! Listen up Dre, my nigga...get all that info about them triggers that cause you to stress and not be your best. Find out right now how you can transform a trigger into a positive experience, creating distance between the actions of your flesh and the thoughts in your mind. Find a way to stay in tune in this class... so that your ass don't end up back in the hood when things don't go so good in your life, so you can keep the peace with your wife, so you can manage stress and strife with a smile! Just get through the class and after a while, it'll all be over. Yeah, two o'clock comes real fast, then class is over...well at least until next week!

Well, we are quickly approaching the end of this book because I have decided to write The Heart of A Pastor, The Pen of A Man...Volume 2, therefore I must save some of the Poems for my next book! But don't worry, I will share with you a few more before the end. As a matter of fact, the next poem that I want to share with you is about a subject matter that I have found to be very disturbing. Now before I begin, let me just say this, I am a firm believer that God will often times use Doctors and medications to bring about healing for our minds and our bodies! Having said that, I want to put out this disclaimer that I am in no way, shape or form, encouraging or suggesting to anyone to stop taking, or refuse medication after reading this book, especially this next poem. This poem contains my thoughts, feelings and opinion about the overall general mindset of the Pharmaceutical Companies at large. I can honestly say that at my worst, which was when I was admitted into the program, the medications that I was prescribed and took helped me tremendously! PTSD depression is unlike any other form of depression known to mankind, and without the stabilization that I received from the medication, I don't think that I would be here today, let alone to be able to focus and concentrate long enough to write a book! So, to those of you that are now taking a shitload of meds, cheer up, it does get better! And let me add this, do not be afraid to ask to have your meds titrated down after awhile. There is nothing wrong with asking for a lower dose, just don't try to do it on your own, or stop taking them when you feel better, because the truth is that you're feeling better because you're taking meds, and that's REAL TALK! This poem is entitled **"Arrest The Med Makers"**…Enjoy, and remember, it's just my opinion!

Arrest The Med Makers

White collar criminals, painting subliminal pictures in your mind, with commercials saying this med is fine, this med is helpful…but I remain skeptical and not moved because most of these meds have never been FDA approved. Meds to keep you "grooving" legally by repeating the same dose three times daily…I'm not okay, I'm not okay with popping this pill! It's not a thrill because it can kill me if I'm not careful…My mailbox full of samples of these meds that were tested by some random blind study...Bloody becomes the liver and organs that these meds affect, habitual intake has upset the digestion process that takes place in the kidneys...Are you kidding me? Why didn't Socrates with his smart ass put the side effects of these meds in a book? He probably did, but the makers of these meds took a second look at the amount of profit they were making off of these meds...Yeah, they probably said "we'll keep selling them, making them at one hundred percent, then just label the bottles with a small ass print of warning...They won't read it anyway, then we'll be okay with our legalized, slow working murders." You never heard of levies being processed against the testing of meds, until countless numbers of people end up dead, on some machine, in some hospital, trying and giving their all to recuperate...Having the attitude and fortitude of the champion L.A. Lakers, when all of this could have been avoided if there was an arrest of the greedy med makers! Yeah, it's definitely time to arrest, judge, sentence and imprison the Greedy White Collared Med Makers...Before it's too late!

Got pretty deep on that one, huh? Lol, yeah, I know. I was really feeling some type of way about the side effects of those meds, but in the end, it worked out for my good! What really helped me though was that I began to change my eating habits, and I found out that I was able to get more natural nutrients inside of my body which did help me with a lot of anxiety! Eating healthy will always help you to feel better, regardless of how much or little medication that you may be taking right now!

The last two poems that I am going to share with you in this book will be monumental for you, just as they were for me! The first one deals with War. Yeah, for just a moment, we are going to visit that terrible, ugly place called the battlefield. It is important to visit it on paper, so that you can free it from your mind, to reveal the true, new you! It might be painful to read, because for some of you, you experienced worst than this, but keep reading to break free. Listen, if you feel like crying, cry. If you feel like yelling, scream into a pillow. If you begin to shake or tremble from fear, it is okay, because though you may just be holding a book in your hands with words written on a page, please understand that I am right there going through with you, to lead you out of that place of torment. More importantly, God is there, and He promises that He will never leave you or forsake you! You made it home for a reason! He kept you alive because you have a destiny to fulfill! You are a great person, despite anything that you've ever done! Your life matters and you are important! Because of your sacrifice, today many people are alive! Because you were willing to kill and willing to die, millions will be able to enjoy freedom for years to come! You may never get all of the accolades, help, healthcare, ratings, or benefits that you deserve while here on earth, but you can bet your bottom dollar of this one thing…God has not forgotten your sacrifice or your struggles, and He will reward you sure enough one day. If not here on earth, then definitely in Heaven, because you are the closest person to Jesus' likeness here on earth! You may not think so but get this, Jesus gave his life for the ransom of many. He died so that others could be free! He fought a battle that wasn't even His to fight to begin with…Sound familiar? Right! So to you beloveds, I salute you, now let's reminisce for a moment, and then accept our reality!

The Person Behind The Trigger

Flash Bomb, fast moving to take my position…I'm in theatre on a mission with my M16A1 pointing at an empty window. Crouched down so low that I'm only visible to my squad, and although it's hard to continue to hold this position, my vision is crystal clear…a shadow appears in the window, POP, POP, and now its no longer there. I'm now amidst a sea of screams… People screaming…moving forward is my team and, more shooting, more killing, go figure…I'm just the person behind the trigger following orders. Now back in society, I'm on the border of insanity! Mind shaking, pain staking pain in my brain, it's still raining bullets...Who can forget the shots that rang out and sprang out of the end of my weapon. Rushing in, stepping over dead bodies to secure a territory, not ever telling the full story because it hurts so much...Won't touch the emotions that are connected to this because to me, its much bigger than life. Yeah, its much, much bigger...Why? Because I, I was the person behind the trigger firing nonstop to guarantee my survival...Pulling my trigger at my rival! Yeah, pulling my trigger at my rival! The shooting won't end or rescind until me and my friends make it out safely! Yeah, I'm pulling the trigger until we make it home...I just want to make it back home!

Well, I made it home, and if you're reading this book, then that means you made it home also! Now smile, even if tears are streaming down your face right now, smile, because everything will be okay! You will get better, your family, marriage, and mind, will be restored! You are more than a conqueror, God says so in His Word! You will make it! I decree and declare over your life right now that no weapon formed against you shall prosper! Everything that you lost out of yourself on the battlefield, you will recover! Your BEST days are ahead of

You! Your addiction is defeated! You will have victory and success in every area of your life! Keep fighting the good fight of Faith! You are a Winner, and Angels surround You! You are precious cargo, and there are wells of life getting ready to burst forth out of You! This Beloved, is who you are, so just accept it! It will never change, this IS who YOU are! Now, let me tell you, who I am! Despite the sometimes use of "strong" language in this book, despite some of the "angry" poetry, despite what many will think or say about me after reading this book, this is who I am! So if anyone asks you, who am I, bring them to this poem!

Who Am I?

Who am I? I'm this wonderful guy, that did not die, that often cries about my past…These feelings of guilt, pain and hurt come up fast, and they last all day long. The songs that I sing don't bring me joy anymore like they did before…Now I explore the core of the six foot four frame that I call me. I take a deep breath and release a sigh, and I'm going to attempt to answer the question, who the hell am I?

Who am I? I am this wonderful guy, that did not die, that often cries about my past…I did not die, I am a wonderful guy, and I often cry about my past...Yeah, about my past I cry, I did not die, and I'm a wonderful guy...I am fearfully and wonderfully made!

God played a huge part in my success, I am the best and only me that was ever created...My identity, as I have stated before is wonderful! Full of wonder and splendor with no end...God is my best friend, and at the end of the day, I can honestly say, that I love who I am! Yeah, Who am I? I'm a wonderful guy, that did not die, that often cries about A past...But I will not let it affect my future! At the end of the day, I love who I am because God made me, who I am...Now argue with that!

But just in case you missed it, you know, who I really am, let me give it to you one more time, so you can really feel what I'm saying!

Can You Feel Me?

Tall, Dark and Handsome...I would pay a ransom for myself of a million dollars or more...As I have said it so many times before, my past pains preceded my powerful present, which then pushes me into my prominent future! So, shoot your mouth off about me all that you want to, but keep watching because the greatness of my future will definitely haunt you for the rest of your life! Excuse me Sir, excuse me Ma'am, can you feel me? Do you feel what I'm saying? While you're Axe(ing) it, I'm spraying down with Polo Black and "Macking" it...Exactly, not sporadically, but purposeful with each release of the button... I'm schooling you right now, so think of me like E.F. Hutton. Just stand, listen and take it all in...Stay put, even though you don't feel like staying, because it's really worth your while. Unclog your ears, smile, and shelve your emotions for just a moment...Can you feel me? Do you feel what I'm saying? Check this out, basically this is really all that I'm trying to say...Today, yeah today I'm okay with the way that this day is the day that The Lord has made just for me! You may not agree, or see what I see, but I'm free! Yes, I'm free to be me on the land, in the sea, from the Redwood Forest to the shores of Tripoli...Yeah, today I'm free, and I love me, and it feels Real Good!! Now can you feel me? Can you feel what I'm saying?

Thank you for reading, thank you for sharing this book with others, but most importantly, thank you for allowing me to share my Heart and Pen with You! May God's love lead and guide you each and everyday, and may His peace find its way into your Hearts! I love you, yeah, Pastor Andre loves you, God loves You, and now make sure that not another day passes without You loving Yourself! I'm going to get started on volume 2!! Peace!!!

Just so you know how Awesome God Is, I will be receiving my double B.A. Degree next month; B.A. in Theology and B.A. in Pastoral Counseling.

My son Marcus will be graduating from Delaware State University with a B.A. in Business, and my son Marvin was selected and honored as a National Honor Society Member this year. So you see, that in the midst of any "mess", God can make mircles! Never Stop Believing!!!

ABOUT THE AUTHOR

Andre L. Smith was born and raised in Yonkers, New York. He is Combat Veteran of Desert Storm, a father of Three, Founder and Pastor of **Down To Earth Ministries, located at 123 Fifth Street, Delaware City Delaware 19706**.

He resides in Newark, Delaware with his beautiful wife, Dana S. Smith and son Marvin. Anything else you want to know about him, contact him yourself!

(Lol) Real Talk! 302.464.9603 or PastorA.dte.as@gmail.com

Me and My Baby!!!

www.ingramcontent.com/pod-product-compliance
Lightning Source LLC
Chambersburg PA
CBHW072112290426
44110CB00014B/1891